T0032054

WILD WHEELS!

Hottest Muscle Cars

By Bob Woods

Enslow Publishers, Inc.
40 Industrial Road
Box 398
Berkeley Heights, NJ 07922
USA
http://www.enslow.com

Library of Congress Cataloging-in-Publication Data

Woods, Bob.
  Hottest muscle cars / by Bob Woods.
    p. cm. — (Wild wheels!)
  Summary: "Read about the beginning of America's love for muscle cars, and see
why they are still loved today"—Provided by publisher.
  Includes bibliographical references and index.
  ISBN-13: 978-0-7660-2872-2 (library edition)
  ISBN-10: 0-7660-2872-0 (library edition)
  1. Muscle cars—United States—Juvenile literature. I. Title.
  TL23.W66 2008
  629.222—dc22

                              2007007423

ISBN-13: 978-0-7660-3611-6 (paperback)
ISBN-10: 0-7660-3611-1 (paperback)

Printed in the United States of America

10 9 8 7 6 5 4

To Our Readers: We have done our best to make sure that all Internet Addresses in
this book were active and appropriate when we went to press. However, the author
and publisher have no control over and assume no liability for the material available
on those Internet sites or on other Web sites they may link to. Any comments or
suggestions can be sent by e-mail to comments@enslow.com or to the address on the
back cover.

Cover Photo: Alamy/Transtock, Inc. **Back cover:** Ron
Kimball/www.ronkimballstock.com

Interior Photos: Alamy/John Lamm, pp. 1, 35 (bottom); Alamy/Motoring Picture
Library, pp. 22–23, 35 (top); Alamy/Simone Romeo, pp. 1, 27; Alamy/Mark Scheuern,
pp. 42, 43; Alamy/Guy Spangenberg, p. 17; Alamy/Phil Talbot, pp. 3, 8, 35 (middle), 40;
Alamy/ Transtock Inc., pp. 3, 14, 20, 31; Associated Press, p. 25; AP/John T. Barr,
p. 26; AP/Darron Cummings, p. 34–35; AP/Richard Drew, p. 38; AP/Carlos Osorio,
pp. 3, 7, 32; AP/Wayne Scarberry pp. 3, 36–37; Auto Imagery, p. 4–5; Courtesy of Ford
Motor Company, p. 18–19; Courtesy Volo Auto Museum, Volo, IL., p. 9; Ron Kimball/
www.ronkimballstock.com, pp. 1, 3, 12–13, 16, 28, 30, 44; Motorace Graphiks/Adrian
Ketchum, p. 11.

Contents

CHAPTER 1

The Need for Speed

The crowd went crazy as the two cars raced around the track. The experienced driver of the speeding "Bullet" was the favorite to win. Sure enough, he had been in the lead for the entire race. But then the rookie behind the wheel of the other car, the "Sweepstakes," began to catch up.

Ford-built race cars have come a long way since Henry Ford's victory with the "Sweepstakes" in 1901. This Ford Mustang drag racing car is being driven by John Force in 2007.

The race was now down to two laps. In front of thousands of cheering fans the underdog pulled ahead. The Bullet's engine had almost three times as much power as the Sweepstakes', but it ran badly toward the end. The Sweepstakes and its first-time driver stayed in the lead and won easily. It was a huge upset. The more powerful car driven by a more experienced driver had lost to a rookie!

That famous race is amazing not only for its come-from-behind finish by an unknown driver. What is also incredible is the fact that it took place more than 100 years ago, on October 10, 1901! The race is important in America's long history of hot cars and auto racing.

It was run on a mile-long dirt track in Grosse Pointe, Michigan. Alexander Winton, the driver of the Bullet, was the favorite to win. He owned a successful car manufacturing company. He was also one of the best-known race car drivers in what then was a brand-new sport.

Winton's challenger was another auto pioneer, Henry Ford. Ford had built a car called a "quadricycle" in 1896 and started the Detroit Automobile Company. The company had flopped, but Ford knew that the automobile would eventually catch on in the United States.

Ford decided to build a race car, the Sweepstakes. It had a two-cylinder engine and Ford claimed that it could reach 72 miles per hour (mph). That does not seem fast for a race car, but in 1901, the world speed record for automobiles was just under 66 mph.

WILD FACT

A cylinder is one of the main parts of a car's engine. Inside it are moving parts that produce power to turn the wheels. Most of the engines in today's cars have between four and eight cylinders. Usually, more cylinders equals more power.

NASCAR driver Dale Jarrett (right) rides in a replica of Henry Ford's Sweepstakes race car. The original Sweepstakes is in the Henry Ford Museum in Dearborn, Michigan.

In 1903 Henry Ford founded the Ford Motor Company. That company has become one of the world's leading car manufacturers and is still a big name in auto racing. Over the years, Ford has made some of America's hottest cars, including the Thunderbird and the Mustang.

Like Ford, many other companies developed cars through racing. People figured that a car that did well at the racetrack would be good on the street, too. "Win on Sunday, sell on Monday" became a popular saying.

The Dodge Charger was one car that became popular with consumers because of its success in National Association of Stock Car Auto Racing (NASCAR) events.

The Charger is also one of the most famous "muscle cars." Muscle cars were introduced in the 1960s by U.S. automakers. They were a big hit with car-crazy "motorheads." Super-fast muscle cars had powerful engines and cool designs. They

The 1968 Dodge Charger was everything a muscle car should be—fast, midsize, affordable, and most of all, cool!

The Chevy Camaro was a popular muscle car that also did well on the racetrack. This is the 1969 model.

were also affordable. Admired on public streets, they were winners at the track, too. Besides the Charger, other muscle cars include the Mustang, Pontiac GTO, Chevy Camaro, and Dodge Challenger.

The original muscle car era ended around 1975 as car manufacturers began to make smaller, fuel-efficient cars. A worldwide gasoline shortage and anti-pollution laws in the mid-1970s forced car companies to make less-powerful muscle cars. Because of that, fewer muscle cars were sold. People did not seem to want to buy a "muscle" car that did not have much "muscle."

Muscle cars did not go away, though. Owners continued to love and drive them, and the market for used muscle cars remained very strong. Today, it is not unusual to see price tags of $100,000 or more on muscle cars from the 1960s and 1970s that are in excellent condition. In 2006, a 1970 Plymouth Barracuda convertible was bought at an auction for $2,160,000!

The Internet has created a huge network of buyers and sellers of muscle cars, as well as owners looking for parts and accessories. Restoring old models to their original condition is a popular hobby. Shows around the country featuring these so-called classic cars are filled with shining muscle cars.

The car companies have noticed the ongoing popularity of muscle cars. Beginning in the early 2000s, they introduced a new breed of high-performance muscle cars. Some are updated versions of the classics. Pontiac released a new GTO, Dodge came out

Classic car shows are a great place to get up close and personal with muscle cars. This one is at Watkins Glen International raceway in New York.

with a new Charger and Challenger, and the Ford Mustang has enjoyed a successful comeback. An all-new Chevy Camaro is also scheduled for release in 2008.

Any one of them would easily leave Henry Ford's Sweepstakes in the dust. Yet that two-cylinder winner deserves a special place in history as the ancestor of America's muscle cars.

CHAPTER 2

The "Goat"

There was a popular song in 1964 that declared, "I'm the coolest thing around." The song was "GTO" by Ronnie and the Daytonas. In 1964, the Pontiac GTO was one of the coolest cars around. Not only was the 1964 GTO cool enough to be included in a song's lyrics, but it was the first muscle car.

The Pontiac GTO came along at the right time. Drivers—especially young ones—wanted something different and exciting. Most could not afford expensive, full-size luxury cars, like Lincolns or Cadillacs.

They were too big and slow, anyway. Foreign sports cars, such as models from MG, Triumph, Austin-Healey, and Porsche, were nice, but they were expensive and small, with just two seats. Young drivers wanted something different and cool, but more affordable and roomy, just for them.

The GTO was totally cool. It was a "high-performance" car. High-performance cars are fun to drive, have big, powerful engines, go fast, and handle well in curves and tight turns. The GTO was a midsize (medium-sized), two-door model. It was offered as either a hardtop or a convertible for about $3,500 (this is equivalent to about $21,000 today).

WILD FACT

Cubic inches are the units used to measure the size of a car's engine. In most cases, more cubic inches means more power.

This V-8 engine is from a 2004 GTO. The valve covers that say "GTO" form the top of the "V." Under each valve cover are four cylinders.

The name "GTO" was borrowed from an Italian sports car, the Ferrari GTO. GTO stood for *Gran Turismo Omologato* (Italian for "Grand Touring Homologated." Homologated means that a car model has been officially approved for racing). American fans soon nicknamed the speedy Pontiac the "Goat."

It came with a 389-cubic-inch V-8 engine, dual (two) exhaust pipes, a three-speed manual transmission (gears powered by the engine to turn the wheels), and premium tires. It could rocket from 0 to 60 mph in 7.5 seconds—faster than many of today's cars! From a standstill, the GTO could complete a quarter-mile straightaway in 15.7 seconds, reaching a blazing speed of 92 mph.

At first, Pontiac was not sure how well the GTO would sell. The company decided to make only 5,000 to start. To their surprise, the 1964 Goat was an instant hit. Eventually 32,450 were produced and sold that year.

The GTO helped launch the muscle car era. Over the next decade, Pontiac was joined by Ford, Chevy, Plymouth, and Dodge in producing muscular models. All of these cars had powerful engines and flashy looks. But GTO lovers knew that the "Goat" was the original muscle car. Even with all those other machines on the road alongside it, the GTO was still the coolest thing around.

WILD FACT

A V–8 engine is an eight–cylinder engine with two sets of four cylinders lined up alongside each other in a "V" shape.

The Pontiac GTO went through many changes from 1964 until 1974, the last year it was produced. The 1965 model "grew" more than three inches in length. The position of the headlights changed, too. In 1966, the GTO featured curved rear fenders (the body parts that surround the wheels). These were called "Coke-bottles" because of their shape.

In 1969, buyers could select a higher-priced version called "The Judge." It was named after a comedy routine from *Rowan & Martin's Laugh-In*, a popular television show at the time. For an extra $337, Judge owners got a bigger engine, fancier wheels, wider tires, and a rear spoiler (a wing-like device that helps a car handle better at high speeds).

Because of the gas shortage and the new anti-pollution laws, the 1974 GTO was not so "muscular." Nevertheless, it was the final model of a great car dynasty.

1966 GTO

2004 GTO

Who says you can't teach an old Goat new tricks? In 2004, 30 years after the last GTO roared, Pontiac rolled out a brand new beast. The original muscle car was back on America's streets.

True to its legendary roots, the curvy, two-door speedster had a mighty V-8 engine under the hood. The new Goat could zip from 0 to 60 mph in 5.3 seconds and reach a top speed of 155 mph!

The 2005 and 2006 GTOs offered more of the same speed and appeal, with slight changes each year. The '05 model had an air scoop (which brings in outside air to help keep the engine cool) on the hood and a bigger engine. In 2006, buyers could choose between two new colors, Brazen Orange or Spice Red.

CHAPTER 3

Pony Tale

Around the same time the GTO was heating up the highways, Ford was about to unleash a hot new car of its own. And there was no better place to show off a whole new type of car than at the 1964 World's Fair in New York City. There, millions of people would see amazing new technology such as computers, robots, and microwave ovens. They would also see the Ford Mustang for the first time.

The 1964 Ford Mustang was an instant hit. People loved its sporty looks, the power of the optional V-8 engine—and the affordable price tag!

On April 13, Ford showed a gleaming white convertible with bright red bucket seats at the fair. The car had a galloping chrome stallion on the front grille. It was called the Mustang. Later, TV networks started running a commercial about the new Ford. It announced that the Mustang was coming to dealers' showrooms on April 17.

Within a week, more than four million people had flocked to dealers to see the Mustang. Thirty thousand orders were taken for "the pony car," as it was quickly nicknamed. The Mustang would go on to

WILD FACT

Besides the "horse" connection to the Mustang name, the term "pony car" came to mean any compact, sporty model like the Mustang. Pony cars with high-performance engines were also considered muscle cars. They included versions of the Plymouth Barracuda, Chevy Camaro, and Pontiac Firebird.

The 1965 Mustang had a more powerful engine and a racy-looking fastback (sloping rear windshield). These features helped it to compete with other muscle cars.

become one of the most popular, successful, and hottest American cars of all time.

The first Mustang had a unique, sporty exterior, and was available as a convertible or a hardtop. It had a six-cylinder engine and a three-speed manual transmission. It was inexpensive, starting at around $2,400 (this is roughly $14,500 in today's money). It attracted young buyers, mostly women. (In fact, according to a Ford spokesperson, half of the eight million Mustangs sold since 1964 have been bought by women.) To appeal to fast-driving guys, a 289-cubic-inch V-8 engine was available to add muscle to the pony.

The more powerful Mustang turned out to be much more popular. Many owners wanted to keep up with the GTO and the sporty Chevy Corvette, both on the road and the racetrack. That led Ford to take it up another notch by introducing high-performance models in 1965. One of these was a racy 2+2 fastback with a 271-horsepower (hp) engine. (The 2+2 meant that it had two front seats and two small back seats. The "fastback" referred to a sporty-looking sloped back windshield.)

WILD FACT

Horsepower is a measure of engine performance. It compares the power created by one horse to what an engine can do. For example, it would take 271 horses working together to produce enough power to drive the high–performance 1965 Mustang at top speed!

The company also joined forces with Carroll Shelby, a well-known driver and builder of race cars. Together they came out with the Mustang Shelby GT-350. The street version kicked out 306 hp. A special race-ready model cranked it up to 360 hp.

Over the next several years, the Mustang continued to grow in size, power, and variety. In 1969, the Mach 1 and Boss models were introduced to compete with the Pontiac Firebird, Chevy Camaro, Plymouth Barracuda, and

WILD FACT

It may have been the first "pony" car, but the Mustang was really named after a famous World War II fighter plane, the North American P–51 Mustang.

other muscle cars. These Mustang models had even larger engines.

The 1970s brought more changes, but "smaller" was now the buzzword for all the car manufacturers. The new Mustang II, introduced in 1974, was lighter and more fuel efficient.

Throughout the 1980s and 1990s, Ford continued to make changes to the Mustang. Many of the changes were driven by new automotive technology. More fuel-efficient engines delivered greater horsepower. Lighter bodies and better suspensions helped improve the car's handling at high speeds.

The Mustang was again redesigned for 2005. This time it was made to look more like the most beloved models from the 1960s. Some of the old pony-style muscle was back, too.

The 2007 GT convertible, for instance, features a 300-hp V-8 engine, five-speed manual transmission, and dual exhausts. Options include a ten-speaker stereo system that hooks up to an iPod, a choice of 125 different colors for the dashboard lighting, and 18-inch aluminum wheels with the Pony logo in the center.

WILD

FACT

A car's suspension includes shock absorbers and springs, attached to the wheels, to make the car ride comfortably and steer properly.

The Shelby Rides Again

Mustang fans have always loved the power-packed ponies developed by Ford and race car legend Carroll Shelby. So imagine the excitement when Ford announced that an all-new 2007 Shelby GT 500 would be released. The wait was well worth it. And many felt that the $40,000 price tag was worth it, too!

This 500-hp thoroughbred packs some major muscle. Its supercharged V-8 engine with a six-speed transmission will whip it from zero to 60 mph in 4.5 seconds. As *Road & Track* magazine said: "The GT 500 is ready to rock when you jump on the accelerator."

Fastback to the Future

The 1968 Mustang GT fastback starred in the detective movie *Bullitt,* which was a big hit that same year. Not only was it a totally cool–looking car, but it was driven by one of the coolest movie stars of the day, Steve McQueen. Scenes of his character, Frank Bullitt, chasing bad guys up and down the streets of San Francisco made moviegoers' hearts beat faster.

In 2001, to celebrate the movie and the late McQueen, Ford built 5,000 special Bullitt Mustang GTs. To make this new model look and drive like the old 1968 original, Ford beefed up the V–8 engine, lowered the suspension, gave it five–spoke wheels, and customized the interior (inside). The cars, which came in blue, black, and dark green, sold out quickly.

For 2005, the Mustang was redesigned to look more like the classic models of the 1960s. This is the 2006 GT.

Today's drivers seem to love Ford's pony car just as much as drivers in the 1960s loved the original. In fact, in 2006, 100,995 Mustangs were sold in just seven months! After more than 40 years, the Mustang remains a proud name and top seller for Ford. And it is still one of America's hottest muscle cars.

CHAPTER 4

Heavy Chevy

Mauri Rose had competed in the famous Indianapolis 500 car race many times before. In 1941, his car had broken down after 60 laps, but then he hopped into another driver's car and won. Rose also had back-to-back Indy 500 victories in 1947 and 1948. Now, on May 30, 1967, he sat at the head of the pack again.

But this time, Rose was not in it to win it. In fact, he was not even driving one of the race cars that compete in the Indy 500. Instead, Rose was behind the wheel of the brand-new Chevy Camaro. The Camaro had been selected as the Indy 500 pace car.

The Camaro had arrived in Chevy dealers' showrooms in September 1966. It was GM's powerful "weapon" in the muscle-car wars being fought by U.S. automakers to make the best and most popular model. The standard Camaro had an inline, six-cylinder engine (cylinders arranged in a straight line, from front to back) with 140 hp. Optional versions, the Rally Sport (RS) and Super Sport (SS), featured flashier looks and V-8 engines that packed plenty of muscle.

There was also a "Z/28" version. It had a four-speed manual transmission and racing

WILD FACT

At the start of an auto race, the pace car leads all the competitors' cars around the track at a certain speed. This is so each race car will be starting from the same speed when the actual race begins. The pace car returns to the track to limit the competitors' speed if there is an accident, bad weather, or debris on the track.

stripes. It also had front disc brakes and power steering—new features at the time. Under the hood was a unique 302-cubic-inch V-8 engine designed for racing. Chevrolet produced 220,906 Camaros that first year, yet only 602 Z/28s. The Z/28 became more and more popular. It was considered the ultimate high-performance Camaro model for years to come.

The popular Z/28 Camaro featured a more powerful engine than the standard version. This is the 1970 model.

Just like other pony cars and muscle cars made during the early 1970s, the Camaro was a powerful road rocket. Its looks changed inside and out from year to year. The engines gained more size and horsepower. Special racing models were designed to compete at

The Ultimate Camaro

No Camaro is more loved by collectors than the 1969 edition. It had a sporty look, but the optional engines really made the '69 Camaro rock.

That year, GM did not put engines larger than 400 cubic inches into any Camaro. They were under pressure from the federal government and consumer-protection groups to produce safer cars. But GM gave permission to certain Chevy dealers to install more powerful engines. That is how a small number of so-called Central Office Production Orders (COPO) Camaros were built and sold in 1969.

The most rare were the 69 COPO Camaros built by an Illinois dealer, who gave them a ZL-1, 427-cubic-inch V-8 engine. Those monstrous machines could generate up to 550 hp. At the time, they were on the expensive side, at $7,200 each. (In today's money, that would be about $38,000.) But hold onto your wallet: In 2006 a collector purchased two of these ZL-1s for $1.2 million each!

This concept Camaro was shown at an auto show in 2006. It got muscle car lovers excited about the possibility of a brand-new Camaro, the first since 2002.

the track. Those cars are highly prized by today's collectors of classic muscle cars.

During the 1980s and 1990s, sales of the Camaro declined. Car companies, including Chevy, were promoting new models with smaller engines that were better on gas. People did not like these Camaro models as much. It was decided that the 2002 Camaro would be the final model.

It happened to be the thirty-fifth year of this great American muscle car, so 3,000 special anniversary SS editions were built. They sported two wide stripes from the nose to the tail, as well as special logos. The final Chevy Camaro rolled off the assembly line on August 27, 2002. Or so everyone thought!

In 2006, General Motors announced that a new Camaro would be introduced in early 2009. Chevy created a buzz in the muscle-car world when it showed off this new, concept Camaro at the 2006 Detroit Auto Show. The silver, ultra-modern model was designed to resemble the 1969 Camaro, the favorite of all the old models. But this sweet ride is totally twenty-first century.

It will be available with either a V-6 or V-8 engine and a manual or automatic transmission. The concept car was powered by a 400-hp LS2 V-8, the standard engine in today's Chevy Corvette.

Will there be a brand-new Camaro pace car at the 2009 Indy 500, 42 years after Mauri Rose's ride around the track? We will have to wait and see.

WILD FACT

Car companies bring their concept cars to major auto shows around the world. These cars are samples of possible future models that the companies may or may not eventually make. So do not get your hopes up—these cool cars are not for sale (yet)!

The Chevy Corvette does not really share the burly looks and tough-guy image of the GTO, Charger, and other classic muscle cars. But when compared to the coolest high-performance cars ever made in the United States, the Corvette runs right alongside them. Serious car lovers consider the "Vette" to be America's original and ultimate sports car.

The Corvette was introduced in 1953. Many feel the 1963 Sting Ray is the coolest 'Vette of all . In 1968, the 'Vette took on the bold look of a mako shark. In the 1980s, the body was made more aerodynamic (to cut through the air more smoothly). By 1996, new technology such as anti-lock brakes (to avoid dangerous skidding) and air bags were standard equipment.

Corvette Z06

The newest generation of Corvettes was introduced in 2006. For owners who can drop $70,000 on a sports car, there is the Z06 'Vette. Those big bucks buy a big LS7 engine, which delivers 500 hp and awesome speed. It can zip through a quarter mile in about 11 seconds, and max out at 190 mph—on a racetrack, of course!

The Chevy Corvette proves that "muscle" comes in all kinds of packages.

Muscle Car or Sports Car?

The original 1953 Corvette

1963 Sting Ray

1968 Mako Shark Corvette

CHAPTER 5

The Fastback Pack

The Dodge Charger was one of the great muscle cars of the late 1960s and early 1970s. It won not only the hearts of many power-hungry, fast-driving owners, but also its share of NASCAR races.

Fast forward to May 14, 2005, and Richmond International Raceway in Virginia.

NASCAR driver Kasey Kahne, in his Number-9 Dodge Charger, battles Tony Stewart during a race on May 14, 2005. Both Kahne and his car proved themselves that day.

Kasey Kahne, one of the popular young drivers in NASCAR's Nextel Cup series, grips the steering wheel of an all-new Charger. He is barreling down a straightaway at about 180 mph!

Dodge had excited muscle-car lovers by reintroducing the legendary Charger in 2005 and showcasing it in Nextel Cup races. No wonder Kahne's loyal fans stood and cheered every time his Number-9 car roared past.

Kahne and the Charger had a lot in common on that Saturday evening at the Chevy American Revolution 400 race. Neither had celebrated a victory yet. The odds were in their favor, though, as the race got underway. Kahne had performed better than any of the 42 other competitors in practice all week.

It was Kahne's second full Nextel Cup season, but he had come close to winning

Muscle car lovers welcomed a new Dodge Charger in 2005, the first one in 27 years. This model, the SRT8, was their favorite.

before. He had finished in second place six times. Would he have to settle for second place again tonight? Or would the Charger mark its first NASCAR win since November 1977 when Neil Bonnett crossed the finish line in first place?

Kahne led the 400-lap race seven different times. He battled back to the front of the pack as the action came down to the last few nail-biting laps. Tony Stewart, one of the very best NASCAR drivers, had been on

Kahne's heels the whole night. The two had exchanged the lead several times.

Stewart and Kahne were side-by-side before Kahne's Charger finally pulled ahead and crossed the finish line just 1.674 seconds ahead of Stewart's Chevy Monte Carlo. "It's an awesome win for everybody on our Dodge Charger race team," Kahne said during an interview. "It's the first win for the Charger, and that's great."

But even if it had not been a NASCAR winner, the new Charger is still a champ. There are six different models, yet muscle-car fans' favorite is the Charger SRT8.

The SRT8 has a raised air scoop on the engine hood, silvery 20-inch wheels, and a rear spoiler. Powering the SRT8 is a 425-hp Hemi V-8 that kicks it up from 0 to 60 mph in a blinding 5.3 seconds. It will hit 100 mph in about 16 seconds!

The story of the Charger's amazing power and speed dates back to January 1, 1966. That is when the first model was unleashed during halftime of college football's Rose Bowl. Millions of Americans watching the game on TV caught their first glimpse of the sporty, two-door fastback. It featured headlights cleverly hidden behind a chrome mesh grille and a taillight that stretched the width of the car.

The big news, though, was under the Charger's hood. One of the optional engines was the awesomely powerful 426 Hemi. The famous Hemi name refers to the unique "hemispherical" (half a sphere) shape of the engine's combustion chamber. This is the internal area of the engine's cylinders where the gas is burned. The Hemi was listed as having 425 hp, but it was actually closer to 500.

To compete against other muscle cars, the Charger underwent design changes during the next few years. The 1968 model had Coke-bottle-shaped rear fenders and

The 1966 Charger was a cool-looking fastback. But the real muscle car appeal was in its incredibly powerful engine.

What Is a Hemi?

The Hemi name became famous when the big, powerful V–8 engine was offered in the original 1966 Charger. In 1964, Chrysler (Dodge's parent company) had put 426–cubic–inch Hemis in their NASCAR race cars. With those engines, the Chryslers swept first, second, and third place! When the Hemi–powered '66 Charger appeared, that race car muscle hit the streets.

What packs the Hemi's incredible punch is the design of the cylinders' combustion chambers, which are dome–shaped at the top. Other engines have flat–top chambers. Gasoline burns much better in the Hemi design. This explains the added power of these engines, and why cars that have them leave others in the dust.

two pairs of round taillights. A racer R/T (road and track) version came with a 440-cubic-inch "Magnum" engine and bumble-bee stripes (two thick stripes in between two thin stripes) on the back end. In 1969, the Charger 500 and Charger Daytona models were introduced. Special versions of both ran in NASCAR races.

By 1974, the Charger, like all muscle cars, had been weakened by government rules requiring cleaner, less powerful engines. The 1974 Charger would be the last high-performance model. Fans were disappointed to see that 1978 would be the Charger's last year. That is, until Kasey Kahne helped the latest version get off to a winning start 27 years later.

Dodge's muscle cars could boast that they were real race cars. After all, their engines, all 426 Hemis like this one, had first been used to power NASCAR vehicles.

The terms "muscle car" and "pony car" have been used to describe some of the hottest cars made by American car companies over the years. Some models fall into more than one category, such as the Camaro and the Mustang. They are considered both

Worthy Challenger

Since the new Charger created so much excitement when it came out in 2005, Dodge decided to bring back another famous name—the Challenger. A concept model was shown at the 2006 Detroit Auto Show. Dodge later announced that the car would go on sale in 2008.

The new Challenger is a stunning, modern version of the original 1970 model. Like the classic model, it will offer an optional Hemi V-8 engine. The two-door will be available as either a hardtop or convertible, and with a manual or automatic transmission. It will also borrow its style from the 1970 model. The '08 Challenger will have floating headlights, ribbed black seats, and a hood with black trim.

The "General Lee" might have been the most famous Charger of all. It was featured in the 1970s TV show The Dukes of Hazzard, *as well as the 2005 movie based on the show.*

pony cars and muscle cars. These stylish, sporty cars do not really share the classic muscle-car image of the GTO and Charger. Others are firmly in one category only, such as the Charger, which is one of the most muscular of the muscle cars.

But no matter what label these cars are given, together they belong in the category of the coolest high-performance cars ever made in the United States.

air scoop—An opening on the hood of a car that lets in air to help cool the engine and helps with engine combustion.

bucket seats—Low front car seats made for one person.

concept car—A car built as a sample of a future design. It may or may not eventually be built for people to buy.

cylinder—Space inside an engine that contains a piston, valves, and other moving parts that supply power to the transmission, which turns the rear wheels of a vehicle.

fastback—A car with a hard top and a back windshield that slopes downward from the back edge of the roof to the rear of the car.

fender—Metal or fiberglass part of a car's body that covers a wheel.

horsepower (hp)—A measure of engine performance and power. It compares the power created by one horse to what an

engine can do. For example, it would take 300 horses working together to create the same power as a 300-hp engine.

pace car—An official car that leads competitors around the track before a car race, and during slowdowns and stops for accidents, bad weather, or debris on the track.

spoiler—A wing-like device attached to the rear of a car that helps it handle better at high speeds.

suspension—A vehicle's system of shock absorbers, springs, and other parts that connect to the wheels to help with steering and to make the ride more comfortable.

transmission—A vehicle's system of gears, powered by the engine, that turn the wheels. With a manual transmission (often called a "stick shift") the driver uses a clutch pedal and changes each gear by hand with a shifter. With an automatic transmission, the gears shift automatically without using a clutch or shifter.

Books

DeLorenzo, Matt. *Mustang 2005: A New Breed of Pony Car.* Osceola, Wis.: Motorbooks, 2004.

Mueller, Mike, with Bob Woods. *Corvette.* Osceola, Wis.: Motorbooks, 2006.

Statham, Steve. *Pontiac GTO: The Great One.* Osceola, Wis.: Motorbooks, 2003.

Zuehlke, Jeffrey. *Muscle Cars.* Minneapolis: Lerner, 2006.

Internet Addresses

http://www.musclecarclub.com Histories and photos of muscle cars.

http://www.musclecarmuseum.com The Web site of a muscle car museum in Tennessee, including a virtual tour and photos of the cars.

http://www.remarkablecars.com Color photos of all types of classic and newer cars. Also has information on car shows, auctions, and museums.

Index